Girl-Swag

A Global Girl's Curriculum for Personal Development & Lifestyle Enhancement

Chloé Taylor Brown

authorHOUSE®

AuthorHouse™
1663 Liberty Drive
Bloomington, IN 47403
www.authorhouse.com
Phone: 1-800-839-8640

Published by AuthorHouse 5/14/2013

ISBN: 978-1-4817-4793-6 (sc)
ISBN: 978-1-4817-4794-3 (hc)
ISBN: 978-1-4817-4795-0 (e)

Library of Congress Control Number: 2013907752

Any people depicted in stock imagery provided by Thinkstock are models, and such images are being used for illustrative purposes only. Certain stock imagery © Thinkstock.

This book is printed on acid-free paper.

Because of the dynamic nature of the Internet, any web addresses or links contained in this book may have changed since publication and may no longer be valid. The views expressed in this work are solely those of the author and do not necessarily reflect the views of the publisher, and the publisher hereby disclaims any responsibility for them.

Cover design by Ms. Benjamin

Girl-Swag: A Global Girl's Curriculum for Personal Development & Lifestyle Enhancement is dedicated to all the girls and young ladies who have extraordinary dreams: those who have aspirations of accomplishing their heart's desire; those who have images of themselves as being excellent; those who want more for themselves, for their families, for their communities, and even for the world.

This workbook is the curriculum for the Global Girl-Swag Initiative. It has been compiled using Chloé Taylor Brown's cutting-edge processes and transformational training techniques from her Personal Excellence Profile—the PEP, her books, *Getting Ready Chloé-Style: Perfecting Your Authentic Image* and *Determine Your Ideal: Creating a Life of Fulfillment and Prosperity*, and from discoveries from working with professional and corporate women.

The processes within this workbook have proven to be dynamic and effective for girls and young ladies, middle school through college, as well as for single adult women, mothers, and women in corporate America.

To book a platinum Girl-Swag symposium, retreat or training workshop for your group please visit www.chloetaylorbrown.com or www.mygirlswag.com.

TABLE OF CONTENTS

ACKNOWLEDGEMENTS

Life is an amazing journey, an adventure that I am extremely blessed to be part of, and so very thankful that I have the ability to think wonderful and excellent thoughts that allow me to live my life by my own design. The process of writing Girl-Swag was spectacular. It is a series of fun, interactive processes and combined chapters that make a real masterpiece when completed. Thank you, God! Thank you, to all who have come into my life and have been a source of encouragement and enlightenment. I appreciate you so very much.

I'm sending love to each of you, today and always,

Chloé

I am very pleased and honored to partner with TV personality, business woman, and former client, Kari Wells. Our goal is to combine our collective knowledge, passion and expertise to inspire, empower and equip other women, young ladies and girls to think differently toward themselves and to develop their assets to create a life of fulfillment and prosperity no matter where they are in life.

Kari's mission is to share, train and coach about The Business of Living for Women and how we can position ourselves to start taking control of our life to create the lifestyle we envision for ourselves and for our families. The Business of Living is about being in charge of your destiny. It is about starting from where you are, today, and putting one foot in front of the other and developing the assets that you now have. It is different for every woman, but it covers all women, no matter where you live, who you are or your age.

When we combine the Global Girl-Swag Initiative, Personal Excellence Coaching and The Business of Living for Women we are truly creating and delivering an excellent blueprint with platinum appeal for women, young ladies and girls.

To connect with Kari please visit
www.KariWells.com

INTRODUCTION

Let's be *real*. Most of us struggle with accepting ourselves, loving our bodies, finding our true identity, connecting with others, and finding purpose in our lives. Or at least we have had this struggle at some point. It seems that a day doesn't go by without hearing people talk about being dissatisfied with themselves or their life situations. Whether it's about their looks, their relationship status, how much money is in their pocket, or how popular they are, people just don't seem to be all that satisfied with themselves these days. Let's face it, not only do magazines and commercials bombard us with the "ideal" image of beauty, money, and popularity, but now we have reality TV replacing family shows, documentaries, and comedies with programs and advertisements that are completely *unreal*, while pretending to "be" real. Imagine, you can go on a TV show and within a few weeks, you can lose a hundred pounds, find the love of your life, and turn into a beauty queen. Now, is that real? No it's not! Unfortunately, some people aim for "perfection" in their lives instead of valuing who they are and uncovering their authenticity. What do I mean by authenticity? Authenticity means understanding who you are—your *real* self—learning how to let that self shine through, and showing the world how fabulous you truly are. That's authentic!

Since young ladies are constantly faced with these issues in their lives, I decided to write this tell-it-like-it-is book as a preventative measure, not a rehab tactic. And when I say "tell it like it is," I really mean it. I am going to talk to you like I talk to my children, clients, friends, and family. You may find some sarcastic humor in my dialogue, because I am just keeping it *real*!

So if you are an adolescent girl or young lady, and have been dissatisfied with how you feel about yourself, your looks, popularity, your personality, or what you have been able to accomplish in life, then this book is for you. If you are an adult female or a mom, and can relate to feeling this way some time in your life, or you know a young girl who can relate to this, this book is for you, too. These issues touch girls and boys, women and men—all races and ethnicities, religious sectors, socioeconomic classes, athletes....everyone!

My goal in writing this book is to give you tools (coping skills and alternative ways of looking at things) in your toolbox for living a happy and healthy life. I do expect that you will be challenged by certain issues at times in your life; however, when and if you are faced with challenges, you will know how to handle them, and be able to avoid falling into the funky pit of sadness, depression, anxiety, or isolation. After reading and completing this workbook (actually doing the work), you will have the ability and know-how to value yourself, maintain a high level of energy, and be connected to others. I am here to help you appreciate your authenticity, your personality, and your *real* self.

This workbook is a space where you can be completely honest, truthful and open-minded about yourself and how you want to express your authenticity to the world. Completing this workbook is an easy process that you can approach from your creative and playful side. I want this workbook to inspire you and help you recognize that the possibilities for life are limitless. If you are bold and determined enough to stick with this process until the very end, and sprinkle what you have learned into your day-to-day life—every single day—you will be amazed by how exciting you are, and how people will want to connect with you and be on your team...for school, work, business, play...for all of life.

CHAPTER 1
Adore Your Authenticity

Your Body, Your Style, Your Thoughts, and Your Feelings

I'm going to jump right in by saying this: The most important part of having high self-esteem and being a winner in life is to love and value yourself as much as you possibly can. You may be wondering what I mean by adoring your authenticity. Your authentic self is the *true* you. It is who you *really* are. It is your most comfortable self. It is the personality, character, style, and self-image that truly describe you. For this process to really work for you in a big way, you must be honest, original, and open with your thoughts and feelings. In other words, you've got to be yourself, girl—your *real* self. Don't be who you think you should be, who someone else wants you to be, or who you think society expects you to be. Be YOU!

What does Authenticity Mean to Me?

List 6 healthy and positive things you can do to love and value yourself more.

For example: I will be kind and loving to myself when I look in the mirror. I realize that I am unique, and I will appreciate my uniqueness.

1. _____

   _____

   _____

2. _____

   _____

   _____

3. _____

   _____

   _____

4. _____

   _____

   _____

5. _____

   _____

   _____

6. _____

   _____

   _____

List your top 6 authentic traits.

For example: I am a good listener. I like being friends with different people.

1. _____
   _____
   _____

2. _____
   _____
   _____

3. _____
   _____
   _____

4. _____
   _____
   _____

5. _____
   _____
   _____

6. _____
   _____
   _____

Finding Your "Girl-Swag"

I want you to be confident and powerful in all areas of your life and to express yourself authentically—with truthfulness and girl-swag. Girl-Swag is your appearance, your style—the way you present yourself, the goals you have chosen, and the way you feel about yourself. This is important, ladies, because you get to define your own girl-swag. You have the power to choose what thoughts you think, how you feel about yourself, how you feel about your body, who you want as your friends, and what goals you want to set for your life. It's all about you and your natural gifts and abilities. Don't let anybody else define you.

The way you feel about yourself, your body image, your goals, and who you want to become are important. Please know that it is essential that you understand this: The way you speak, behave, look, and dress are important; but, the most important fact to realize is that you are completely unique. There is no one in this universe exactly like you, even if you have an identical twin. You are one-of-a-kind—flawless and beautiful; you already have all the qualities and elements that are necessary to be *you.* You may not have realized this yet. But as you work through this workbook you will start to uncover your "fabulosity" by recognizing what works best for you. You are already an authentic superstar, so let's get busy on shining the spotlight on *you,* darling.

I want you to embrace the uniqueness of your body, your fashion and personality styles, and the individuality of your being. I realize that when you are happy with your body you feel good about yourself. This thing called body image is an essential aspect of your life and your self-expression. We can't ignore it or make it insignificant. Therefore, I am going to help you identify the positive traits and characteristics about your body, your body type, and your body shape and proportions. I'll help you learn to appreciate your genetic and cultural makeup while expressing your authentic self—through your acceptance and confidence about your body, your fashion style, and your personality style.

Uncovering Your Personal Girl-Swag

Check the body types, body shapes, and body proportions that fit you the best. If you are an adolescent and still developing, this may be a little tricky for you, so ask an adult to assist you.

Body Types

1. Ectomorphic—tall and thin with long limbs

2. Mesomorphic—athletic and muscular

3. Endomorphic—heavily boned, rounded in appearance, especially around the abdomen

Body Shapes

1. Pear—slim upper body, narrow shoulders, small bust, small waist, voluptuous hips and thighs. This is the most common female shape.

2. Inverted Pear—larger upper body, shoulders 2 or more inches wider than the hips, large bust, and narrow lower body with slim legs and small butt

3. Apple—top heavy, bust and midsection are bigger and wider than your hips, thicker and rounded stomach, abdomen and chest area, with a flat butt

4. Slender—fairly equal measurements of the chest, waist and hips. Straight up-and-down frame with a slightly athletic build.

5. Hourglass—curvaceous, shoulders and hips are balanced, with a well-defined waist

6. Balanced—same size on top and bottom, with a defined waist

Body Proportions

1. Petite—less than five feet and three inches in height

2. Medium—between five feet and three inches and five feet and seven inches in height

3. Tall—between five feet and seven inches and six feet and one inch in height

4. Very Tall—six feet two inches and above in height

Weight

Consider this. The best place to start is by knowing your optimal weight, which is based on your body type, shape, height, frame size, ethnicity, genetics, and age. Know that your body is constantly changing, depending on where you are in your life. Remember, things such as puberty, hormones, stress, sleeping problems, travel, medical issues, anxiety, and depression can cause changes to your weight. Being flexible, patient, and persistent are great personal assets in maintaining a healthy weight range, which is the foundation for optimal energy and living life fabulously. No healthy lifestyle is sustainable if it has given no consideration to a proper eating plan along with fun energetic activity.

Circle the clothing and fashion styles that you like best. Are you...

1. Casual

2. Sporty

3. Conservative

4. Country/Western

5. Bohemian

6. Rebellious/Edgy

7. Urban

8. Chic

9. Sophisticated

10. Glamorous

11. Tomboy

12. Nerdy

13. Skater/Surfer

14. Other _____

List your top 2 to 3 styles here in order of personal preference and why:

1. _____

   _____

   _____

2. _____

   _____

   _____

3. _____

   _____

   _____

Circle the personality styles that you feel fit you best:

1. Outgoing/Extrovert

2. Shy/Introvert

3. Funny/Silly

4. Serious

5. Innocent

6. Nerdy

7. Awkward

8. Adventurous/Free-Spirited

9. Artistic

10. Musical

11. Athletic

12. Smart/Studious

13. Other _____

List your top 2 to 3 personality types in order of importance:

1. _____

   _____

   _____

2. _____

_____

_____

3. _____

_____

_____

Defining Your Personal Girl-Swag

For example, Samantha's top 3 fashion styles are chic, sporty, and casual. And her top 3 personality styles are artistic, outgoing, and adventurous. So, Samantha would define her personal girl-swag as a young lady who enjoys the sporty, casual side of life, especially when she is being outgoing and adventurous. However, at times, she expresses her chic, artistic side when she is being cleverly stylish and creative.

Now, combine your top 3 fashion styles with your top 3 personality styles to help define *your* personal girl-swag. Please share your thoughts about why this is your personal girl-swag.

_____

_____

_____

_____

_____

_____

_____

_____

_____

_____

_____

_____

_____

_____

List your top 10 positive attributes/strengths:

For example: I am generous. I am a good athlete. I help out at home. I draw really well. I volunteer in the community. I am a great student. I'm a great singer, etc.

1. _____

_____

_____

2. _____

_____

_____

3. _____

_____

_____

4. _____

_____

_____

5. _____

_____

_____

6. _____

_____

_____

7. _____

_____

_____

8. _____

_____

_____

9. _____

_____

_____

10. _____

_____

_____

Your Thoughts

Imagine this. Our thoughts start off with something as small as a word, an image, or an idea. And we have the ability to turn that small word, image, or idea into something huge and amazing. For example, a young girl may have the idea of learning how to play the guitar. And then she turns that idea into taking guitar lessons, and before you know it, she is playing on stage touring with a band. Or, you may be in French class in school, learning about the French culture. This may spark your interest in learning about their food. And before you know it, you have received a scholarship to attend the Le Cordon Bleu Culinary School in Paris. And that's how *thoughts become things and your reality*. Now, that's amazing!

The fact is, you create your own realities in your mind first. But you have to be confident within yourself—that you are worthy, and that you *can* turn your thoughts into your reality. But, ladies, you have to believe in yourself first! If you don't believe in yourself, your hopes and dreams may not come true. You have to think, believe, and see yourself creating and getting what you want out of school, home, friends, extra-curricular activities, work, and your future.

I want you to get used to the idea of turning your thoughts into reality, creating your own path in life, and achieving your goals in an excellent way—the way that helps you become your personal best.

CHAPTER 2
Perception—Trust Your Gut

Trusting Your Authenticity, Intuition, Instincts, and Gut Feelings

Have you ever heard someone say, "Hindsight is 20-20"? What that means is that after something has occurred you can look back at it and say, "I knew that was going to happen." But unfortunately it's too late for you to do anything about it this time, because it already happened. What you can do is learn from various situations in your life and listen to your intuition, your instincts, and trust your gut.

Remember, you can learn from your mistakes. You can take a good look at the mistakes you or others have made, and recognize what you can do the next time you are faced with a similar situation. That's what I mean when I say, "trust your gut."

You've got to have *in*sight and *fore*sight. Insight is having the ability to see into a situation and look at it from different perspectives. Foresight is the ability to see the consequences of a situation. So if you pay attention to your intuition and your instincts, your gut will tell you what to do. If you have good insight and foresight, then you can trust your gut. Do you see how that works?

Share a time when you used your intuition or your instincts and were able to make a good decision.

Share a time when you were faced with making a decision and you were able to choose wisely because your hindsight was 20-20.

_____

_____

_____

_____

_____

_____

_____

_____

_____

_____

_____

_____

_____

_____

_____

_____

_____

_____

_____

_____

_____

Mind Powers

Did you know that there are three parts to the mind?

1. *Conscious*

2. *Subconscious*

3. *Super-conscious*

All three are like ice, water, clouds, and vapor. They're all one and the same, but they have different functions. However, it's a good idea to sharpen each one of these mind powers, develop them, and use them to help you to maintain your girl-swag so you can have a happier life.

Your conscious mind is the only part of your mind that thinks. It's the part that helps you solve problems, make decisions, and achieve your goals. You can use your conscious mind to choose what thoughts and information enters into your subconscious mind. Many people do not know how to use this power. But this workbook will help you learn how to have *mind power* and to think in a smart, real, and healthy way.

Your subconscious mind is like a computer hard drive that stores everything you've ever thought, said or done, and just like your computer, you have the capacity to retrieve this information at anytime because it is stored in the memory. This is the part of your mind that reminds you of things you may have forgotten. For example, you may not have gotten on a bike for a long time, but when you get back on a bike, you remember how to ride it without thinking about it. That's because it was stored in your subconscious mind. Your subconscious mind also shows how you feel about yourself, others, and situations—noticeable through:

1. Your energy level and mood

2. Your appearance

3. Your body language

4. How you behave and the actions you take

5. Feelings of sadness even though you try to act happy

6. Dressing in a sloppy way that is not typical for you

7. Avoiding eye contact with others

8. Getting into disagreements and arguments with others often

If you have noticed several of these traits showing up in your life, then there is something stored in your subconscious mind that is bothering you. Speak with someone you trust about these areas of confusion, so you can start breaking through to a clear subconscious mind.

Within your subconscious mind lies
the power to change the future direction of your life.
It's up to you what you will create.

Your super-conscious mind gives you life; it is the most important part of the mind, yet the one that most of us know very little about. It is the essence of who you are: your ideals and your purpose in life. It is your *Real Self*—the self that connects with the Giver of all gifts. The super-conscious mind also helps us manage our thoughts, feelings, and behaviors by helping us practice life lessons such as patience, forgiveness, gratitude, kindness, and love. Your most creative expressions and ideas come from the super-conscious mind.

Allowing Your Mind to Work as One

If you want to be the student president of your university, a cheerleader at your high school, organize a bake sale at your middle school, and/or play an instrument in the band, you can use your intelligence (conscious mind power) to see what you want, how you are going to achieve it, and to develop a plan of action. You will also use your gut instinct (subconscious mind power) to help determine which direction to take as you put your plan into action. Lastly, your creative inspirations and life virtues (super-conscious mind) will bring your goals into real life. So, what starts off as a thought becomes a plan that is put into action—and then it becomes the real thing! Isn't that amazing?

What Do You "Perceive" To Be Your Big Goal?

What is *it* that your heart desires—your dream for this month, this year, the next five years, or for the rest of your life—if you can imagine that? This would be your life's purpose. I want you to be crystal-clear about what you want. You are never too young or too old to become clear about what you want and desire for your life. Let's give this a try. Let's start by defining your goal. Put a name on it. Always remember this: If you never clearly define or say what you really want, then you probably will not achieve what you desire; and, even if you do, you will not be able to keep it for a very long period of time.

> *If you are truly intending to be it, to do it, and to make it happen, then the first thing you must do is define it—by naming it.*

Personal Goal

Choose one of your personal goals that you really want to achieve within the next few months. Take some time to really think about this. *For example, "My personal goal right now is to write a book and become a bestselling author." Or, "My personal goal is to be part of my school Yearbook Committee." Or, "My personal goal is to get a college* scholarship." Or, "*My personal goal is to create and manage an online magazine.*"

My personal goal is:

_____

_____

_____

_____

_____

_____

_____

_____

_____

_____

_____

_____

_____

_____

_____

_____

_____

_____

_____

_____

Vision Statement

Write a clear statement as though you are living your goal. *For example, if your goal is to be a writer, your statement could be something like this. "I am having a wonderful time at my book signing party. My friends and family are here and everyone is buying my book! It's a bestseller!"*

Action Steps

Action steps are the steps you are going to take to make your dream a reality. For example: 1) Make a list of things I like to write about. 2) Ask my English and Writing teachers for help. 3) Get advice from someone who has published a book before. 4) Start writing, and don't stop until I am finished.

1. _____

   _____

   _____

2. _____

   _____

   _____

3. _____

   _____

   _____

4. _____

   _____

   _____

Resources

What are my resources? For example: teachers, authors, books, the Internet, the library, bookstores, and people who I can interview.

List your resources below.

1. _____

   _____

   _____

2. _____

   _____

   _____

3. _____

   _____

   _____

4. _____

   _____

   _____

5. _____

   _____

   _____

CHAPTER 3
Decide

Choosing Who You Want To Be: Who am I?
What's My Life's Purpose?

Right now, in this space, you have permission to think really BIG about yourself, darling, without boundaries or restrictions. All limitations have been removed, and there is nothing standing between you and your dreams. You can be, do, and have anything you want. The only thing you have to do is choose what *it* is, to define *it*. What do you really want for your life?

Take some time to consider these life-altering questions. Then record your answers in the **present tense**. Please allow your thoughts to flow effortlessly as you record them here.

Who am I? Your answer to this question is your foundation. It needs to be solid to support your worthwhile life game or games. This is *not* referring to your name, your parents, your favorite subject, or your sport. This is about the essence of your individuality. This is about who you are as a person from the inside out.

I Am...

_____

_____

_____

_____

_____

_____

_____

Who do I want to become?

Don't hold back. This is the time to let your heart's desire spill out. Experience how it might *feel* to be fully immersed in and living your desires right now. Imagine yourself living freely as the *real* you.

I want to become...

_____

_____

_____

_____

_____

_____

_____

_____

_____

_____

What do I want to contribute to my school, neighborhood, family, community, and the world?

Each of us has enormous potential to make huge contributions to the world. We all certainly appreciate Oprah Winfrey, Bill Gates, Tyra Banks, and others for their worldly contributions. But, the good news is they are not the only ones capable of making HUGE life contributions. More exciting news is that this contribution comes out of you being authentic and true to yourself—using your passions, talents, and raw potential. Now, based on the answers you come up with to these powerful questions, you're going to start creating something new and totally amazing in your life.

I want to contribute by...

_____

_____

_____

_____

_____

_____

_____

_____

_____

_____

_____

_____

_____

What are all the things I do really well and like doing?

I do realize that it is hard for many people to recognize their strengths. They feel that if they share their hobbies, gifts, and talents with others, then they are being conceited or bragging about themselves. Well, I am here to tell you that you can love yourself and be confident within yourself without being narcissistic or arrogant. I want you to brag about yourself, darling, and about the things you really do well. This will increase your confidence and help you feel better about what is true about you.

Acknowledge your strengths, and it will allow others to believe in you as well. By being positive and confident, you can become a leader instead of a follower. So go ahead girl, toot your own horn!

I am good at....

_____

_____

_____

_____

_____

_____

_____

_____

_____

_____

_____

What do others consistently compliment me on?

Now don't be shy. Think back to some of the compliments you have received from others, including strangers and people you don't know very well.

I have been complimented on...

_____

_____

_____

_____

_____

_____

_____

_____

_____

_____

_____

_____

Who do I want to become?

This answer may include the type of activities you imagine participating in personally, professionally, and/or in the community. *Who are you being?* What I mean by this is who are you going to show up as in different areas of your life? For example, if you are a dancer, then you have to show up and project yourself with confidence as a dancer, artist, and entertainer. Or, if you are the student government president for your school, then you have to show up and project yourself as a leader and a good listener. I also want you to think about people you admire, and the characteristics and traits they possess as people. What do you admire about them? Now think about what you can take from them, and integrate these into your own personal being and daily habits. Ladies, you CAN become your *best self*!

I want to become...

_____

_____

_____

_____

_____

_____

_____

_____

_____

_____

_____

_____

What do I value?

It is amazing how clear your vision will become when your values are clear. Values can include: self-development, family, spiritual, academic, extra-curricular activities, career, physical/health, community service, relationships, and others. I realize that in our society, many people focus on valuing materialistic things such as houses, cars, clothing, jewelry, shoes, purses, body shape, and the color, length, and style of their hair. But ladies, let's admit it. We know that who *you* really are as individuals is deeper than that. Our values are not the things we see on the outside. So think about it. What do you really value? Be truthful and honest with yourself.

I value...

_____

_____

_____

_____

_____

_____

_____

_____

_____

_____

_____

_____

Now, list these values in the order of what's most important to you.

1. _____

_____

_____

2. _____

   _____

   _____

3. _____

   _____

   _____

4. _____

   _____

   _____

5. _____

   _____

   _____

6. _____

   _____

   _____

7. _____

   _____

   _____

CHAPTER 4

Communicate

Using Your Voice So Others Hear You, Using Your Body So Others See the Real You

Words are powerful! Knowing the right words to say, when to say them, and how to say them are priceless. Communication is a language that speaks volumes. There are two types of communication: verbal and non-verbal.

Verbal communication involves the words you speak, sign language, songs, written words, and the inflection of your voice. The goal of verbal communication is for listeners to get your intended message—to completely understand what you are saying.

Non-verbal communication includes your body language, gestures, your mood, and appearance—including clothing, hairstyles, cosmetics, facial expressions, eye contact, tone of voice, posture and motions, and the position of your body. Did you know that non-verbal communication even includes silence and dance? That's right, ladies, even when you are silent and dancing you are communicating. Isn't communication awesome and liberating?

There are 4 types of non-verbal communication.

1. Poise and Movement

2. Manners and Etiquette

3. Grooming and Cosmetics

4. Clothing and Fashion

Poise and movement

I believe that you project your best image when you demonstrate good posture. Good posture is revered as having confidence and a healthy attitude. It makes you more attractive. It is a wonderful way to feel better about yourself almost instantly—and your body will love you for it! Give it a try! Good posture is not only about sitting and standing up straight, it is about being well adjusted, aligned, balanced, and in symmetry from the top of your head to the bottom of your feet... like a ballerina, or even like a racehorse.

Manners and etiquette

What is a lady? A lady is revered for her polite behavior and refinement. She is the counterpart of a gentleman. She knows how to behave and speak at all times. Refinement is achieved through good manners, which are rules that set a standard of behavior—like showing respect for others, being kind, polite, and considerate. Every lady, regardless of her age or background, should be educated and taught the importance of good manners and proper etiquette, which go hand in hand. Are you a lady?

Etiquette is about using your manners (behaviors) so that you are comfortable with yourself, and, as a result, you are able to make those around you feel comfortable as well (you build rapport). It's about knowing the rules and knowing when it's okay to break them so as not to humiliate others. When you are gracious, thoughtful, and kind, other people are attracted to you. Have you ever seen a girl or young lady who was pretty and looked awesome in her clothes? But, when she opened her mouth to speak, you discovered her words did not match your impression of her? You realized she did not seem to have good manners or etiquette. What was your impression of her before she spoke?

_____

_____

_____

_____

_____

_____

_____

What was your impression of her after she spoke and you learned that she did not practice proper etiquette?

_____

_____

_____

_____

_____

_____

_____

The way you present yourself and communicate with others can set you apart and give you:

The 5 C's:

1. Confidence

2. Character

3. Credibility

4. Connection to others

5. Charisma

Without proper communication skills, your presentation style and communication can also destroy your chances of having high self-esteem, being taken sincerely, being respected, doing your best, and making friends. Keep in mind, using your voice effectively can be a reliable and legitimate way to present yourself to the world—authentically.

Did you know that approximately 7% of how others may perceive you is communicated verbally? About 40% is through your tone of voice, and about 55% is communicated non-verbally.

Connecting Body Image, Fashion, and Self-Esteem

Usually, when we refer to a person's appearance we naturally think of the way she looks or the clothes or fashions she may be wearing. But there is more to it than that. Because fashion, body image, and self-esteem are so interconnected, it is essential that you understand that clothing and fashion are often thought of as an extension of who you are as a human being. Now, we know that sounds silly, but it is true. Many people look at the clothes and the fashions that you wear as *"you,"* and as a central part of body image. Because of this, unconsciously, in the body-fashion-self-esteem interaction, you experience something inside of yourself called the *Selfing Process.*

The Selfing Process

The *Selfing Process* is the communication of the self, which allows you to "put *IT* on." What do I mean by "put *IT* on"? I mean that whatever you want people to think about you, feel about you, and believe about you, you can actually "put IT on." For example, if you want people to believe that you are the next American Idol, you would not only have to have the ability to communicate verbally, with a fabulous voice, but you would also have to create the identity of a singer and entertainer, and put IT on *YOU.* That's called the "IT" factor.

The "IT" factor is the je ne sais quoi, or that indefinable "something" that sets you apart from others, and makes you special, unique, and authentic.

You may have heard judges on shows like *American Idol* or *America's Next Top Model* tell certain contestants that they have this. Those are the contestants that make it to the finals, and the one with the "IT" factor takes home the grand prize. That could be you too, darling!

This process includes five layers of getting ready and work harmoniously together. Keep in mind that the necessary prerequisites are respecting, liking and loving yourself.

The five layers of the Selfing Process include:

1. Verbal communication

2. Poise and movement

3. Manners and etiquette

4. Grooming and cosmetics

5. Clothing and fashion

The following questions will help you recognize your communication skills and determine areas that may need some improvement. Take some time to answer the following questions. Now I don't need to remind you to be open and honest, do I? To answer these questions, it's okay if you ask others for their opinions.

1. Is the quality of my voice clear and understandable? (Yes/No) How do I think my voice sounds to others?

_____

_____

_____

_____

_____

_____

2. Can I turn the volume of my voice up or down? (Yes/No) When would it be appropriate to turn my volume up or down?

_____

_____

_____

_____

_____

_____

_____

3. Do I speak too fast? (Yes/No) Do people ask me to repeat myself (Yes/No)? If so, how can I improve this?

_____

_____

_____

_____

_____

_____

4. Do I speak too slowly, leaving others wanting to complete my sentences for me? (Yes/No) If so, how can I improve this?

_____

_____

_____

_____

_____

5. Do I use a lot of dialect and slang when I speak? (Yes/No) If so, how might this be perceived by others? Can this negatively affect their impression of me?

_____

_____

_____

_____

_____

Your Communication Goals

Now that you have been able to determine your communication skills, let's set some new communication goals. What are some things you would like to work on so that you can use your voice to attract healthy friendships, fun opportunities, and to express the *real* you?

Here are some examples to get you started:

1. To enhance my verbal and non-verbal skills

2. To appear intelligent and confident

3. To be energetic and expressive

4. To paint pictures with my words

5. To use colorful words that express my feelings

6. To make sure my message is not distorted, misunderstood or ignored

Now, it's your turn to come up with your goals:

_____

_____

_____

_____

_____

_____

_____

_____

CHAPTER 5

Build Rapport

Respect Yourself and Your Peers

Have you ever met someone and instantly you knew you would be friends for a lifetime? If you have experienced this, then you know what *rapport* feels like. Rapport is when you have a great relationship and harmony with someone. If you have wonderful rapport with someone, then you feel connected and comfortable with that person. Many of us have experienced times when we felt that we did not have rapport with someone. But don't worry; there are steps you can take to learn how to connect with just about anyone. The foundation and prerequisite for building great rapport is to love and respect yourself, to respect your peers, and to be a good communicator. So, hopefully you paid attention to chapter four's discussion of verbal and non-verbal communication styles. Now, let's give it a try.

10 quick and easy steps to building rapport:

1. Respecting others' viewpoints, values, and beliefs

2. Giving eye contact

3. Truly listening to what the other person is saying and showing empathy

4. Finding areas of interest and commonality with the other person

5. Acting like you already have rapport with the other person

6. Showing interest in what the other person is saying

7. Using appropriate movement and gestures

8. Not interrupting others

9. Sharing your thoughts and feelings

10. Being your authentic self

Body Awareness

You may not realize this, but your body language is a very important part of building rapport. How you move your body, the *gestures* you make, and even your posture—each sends a message about what you feel and how you feel about yourself, as well as what type of friend you may be.

Poise and posture can be put to the test by walking.

The key to grace and elegance of *movement* when walking is that it must be perfectly natural. Each person has a distinct walk; however, my goal is to help you relax in your own walk, to perfect it through poise, posture, and grace. Think of a racehorse. You must learn to move with the same grace, elegance, and coordination. Every girl and woman has the ability to walk like a high-fashion runway model; it has nothing to do with your height, weight, or size, but everything to do with how you feel about yourself and what your body language is expressing.

Keep this in mind. Your body language is a representation of how you feel about yourself. So, be aware of your body and the messages it is sending to others.

The all-time universal facial expression is a smile.

Gestures can be a wonderful way to assist you in communicating your feelings and what you are thinking. They can help make your conversations more animated and exciting. However, it is also important to realize that gestures can be misleading if you do not have *body awareness*.

Inappropriate body language includes body language that does not match the verbal language. Your gestures and movement should match the situation and the verbal statements. For example, if you are telling a friend that you failed a class and you are worried about what your parents are going to say, but you are smiling and laughing, then you are showing inappropriate body language, which can be confusing to your friend—who will wonder whether you are truly worried or if you are actually joking about failing the class.

Exercise: Using the 10 steps to building rapport, think of situations in your life where you can use these steps to build rapport with someone. Write your examples below.

1.   Respecting others' viewpoints, values, and beliefs

Example: I will learn more about my new friend's religious beliefs, and share mine with her.

_____

_____

_____

_____

_____

_____

2. Giving eye contact

Example: *When people are speaking to me, I will give them eye contact instead of texting on my cell phone.*

_____

_____

_____

_____

_____

_____

3. Truly listening to what the other person is saying and showing empathy

Example: *When people are speaking to me, I will let them know that I am paying attention to them by nodding my head and responding to what they are saying. I will also show empathy by trying to put myself "in their shoes."*

_____

_____

_____

_____

_____

_____

4. Finding areas of interest and commonality with the other person—by asking interesting questions and also sharing intriguing parts of yourself

Example: *I will ask my new friend what he/she likes to do for fun, and share what I like to do.*

_____

_____

_____

_____

_____

_____

5. Acting like you already have rapport with the other person

Example: *Think of another person as a friend by inviting that person to eat with me at lunch.*

_____

_____

_____

_____

_____

6. Showing interest in what the other person is saying

Example: *I will ask engaging questions to learn more about the new girl in my class.*

_____

_____

_____

_____

_____

_____

7. Using appropriate movement and gestures

Example: *I will nod my head, smile, laugh, clap, or give a thoughtful touch depending on the situation.*

_____

_____

_____

_____

_____

_____

8. Not interrupting others

Example: *I will not interrupt my friend when she is trying to tell me about her new pet.*

_____

_____

_____

_____

_____

_____

9. Sharing your thoughts and feelings

Example: *I will share my thoughts and feelings more with my friends and family members because I know that they care about me.*

_____

_____

_____

_____

_____

_____

10. Being your authentic self

Example: *Authenticity is being my real, reliable, and genuine self. So, from now on, I will be truthful with myself and let people know the REAL me.*

_____

_____

_____

_____

_____

_____

Now that you have completed your 10 steps to building rapport, you are ready to step out into the world and make better social connections! Let's go, girls!

CHAPTER 6

Interact

Who's On Your Team?

With every major accomplishment, there will be others who will provide support in helping you reach your goals. These individuals are part of your team, and should be considered some of your most valuable resources. Below, list people who are currently on your team, and individuals you would like to be a part of your team to support you in becoming the person of your dreams.

Family:

1. _____

_____

_____

2. _____

_____

_____

3. _____

_____

_____

4. _____

_____

_____

5. _____

_____

_____

School:

1. _____

_____

_____

2. _____

_____

_____

3. _____

_____

_____

4. _____

_____

_____

5. _____

_____

_____

Spiritual:

1. _____

_____

_____

2. _____

_____

_____

3. _____

_____

_____

4. _____

_____

_____

5. _____

_____

_____

Community:

1. _____

_____

_____

2. _____

_____

_____

3. _____

_____

_____

4. _____

_____

_____

5. _____

_____

_____

Health & Fitness:

1. _____

_____

_____

2. _____

_____

_____

3. _____

_____

_____

4. _____

_____

_____

5. _____

_____

_____

Friends:

1. _____

_____

_____

2. _____

_____

_____

3. _____

_____

_____

4. _____

_____

_____

5. _____

_____

_____

Other:

1. _____

_____

_____

2. _____

_____

_____

3. _____

_____

_____

4. _____

_____

_____

5. _____

_____

_____

CHAPTER 7

Act

Lights, Camera, Get Ready for Action!

Success

Success can be created by understanding what you want, knowing who is going to support you, and taking the appropriate actions and necessary steps to get to the outcome that you are trying to achieve. But ladies, you can't do it without having confidence and faith in your ability to succeed. With faith and confidence, come drive, determination, and motivation. In this chapter, I am helping you act upon what you want to accomplish in life. I am going to help you create the steps you can take to succeed in whatever you are passionate about in life.

So, do something, will you?

Before you can create anything worthwhile in your life, *it* must be created and finished in your mind first—that is in your imagination. Determine your vision for your life and start *acting* on it now—right now, by creating and constructing your own holographic vision and vision board. Throughout this incredible process of creating and living your successes, I want you to keep in mind that everything starts and ends in your imagination—in the mind...*your* mind, darling!

That's right, true success of any kind starts in your mind—with an intention. Therefore, *success is creative and not competitive.* So, there is no competition between you and others. No two people on Earth will have the exact same vision, because we are all individual authentic beings.

Exercise:

The steps that you take should be measurable and effective enough to get you to your goal. Let me help you get there. Follow the next steps to help you plan and prepare for your *Steps to Success.*

The Big Picture: Write in detail your heart's desire for what you want to achieve. See it in living color. This will become your holographic vision that will get you excited about what you are working toward, and give you the necessary energy to achieve your dream. A holographic vision is a written document that evokes great feelings of excitement when you read who you are, who you are becoming, and what you are accomplishing and contributing. Take some time to write your holographic vision here in *present tense*, as though it already is real.

_____

_____

_____

_____

_____

_____

_____

_____

_____

_____

_____

_____

_____

_____

_____

_____

_____

_____

_____

_____

_____

_____

Being successful is having the ability and power to manifest your dreams into what you want in your life. Now that you have your holographic vision, I want you to create your "vision board"; in this workbook. Your vision board is your visual image of you, being successful in what you want, as though it is already real. Using words and images from photos, magazines, newspapers, the Internet, and your own creativity, cut and paste your vision on the following pages to create your very own vision board. Even though you may also want to create your vision on an actual board, I want you to complete this exercise here, because this workbook will be your complete *platinum guide—your* blueprint to success and girl-swag. So, I'll call your work in this workbook "Vision Pages"—for three important areas of your life. Please use the next three pages to create your ideal vision.

My Girl-Swag Vision Page

My Girl-Swag Vision Page

.

My Girl-Swag Vision Page

Virtual Living: Creating Your Ideal Life in Your Mind and On Your Girl-Swag Vision Pages

Holographic Visioning: Exercise for Creating Your Ideal Life

Our successful story starts with a thought in our mind. When our stories are in our mind, it is in the virtual state of being. It is up to us to use our body to move us through the steps of success and in the direction of obtaining our dreams. Your body is what holds your physical abilities, gifts, skills, and talents.

Once you recognize that your body is a tool to take action, and to use what you created in your mind and on your vision pages to become a reality, you will be ready to create your ideal life. The following exercises are intended to help you begin to clearly define your ideal life.

Exercise:

1. **What is a typical day like in my ideal life?**

*(Remember, in your ideal life this day is totally amazing. It is excellent! Write everything in **present tense** and be very detailed...using the five senses to evoke the necessary feelings you'll need to manifest your ideal).*

_____

_____

_____

_____

_____

_____

_____

_____

_____

_____

_____

_____

_____

_____

_____

_____

_____

_____

_____

_____

_____

_____

_____

_____

_____

_____

_____

_____

_____

2. What is my family life like in my ideal life?

3. **What type of healthy lifestyle maintenance program will I create and follow for optimal health in my ideal life?**

_____

_____

_____

_____

_____

_____

_____

_____

_____

_____

_____

_____

_____

_____

_____

_____

_____

_____

_____

_____

4. **What type of activities will bring fun and excitement in my ideal life? Why?**

_____

_____

_____

_____

_____

_____

_____

_____

_____

_____

_____

_____

_____

_____

_____

_____

_____

5. **How will I contribute to the empowerment of my family, friends, and community in my ideal life?**

_____

_____

_____

_____

_____

_____

_____

_____

_____

_____

_____

_____

_____

_____

_____

_____

_____

_____

_____

6. **What type of self-improvement activities and classes will I involve myself, in my ideal life? Why?**

7. **What type of friends do I spend time with in my ideal life?**

_____

_____

_____

_____

_____

_____

_____

_____

_____

_____

_____

_____

_____

_____

_____

_____

_____

_____

8. **Where do I see myself after high school or after college or as an adult, based on my ideal life?**

_____

_____

_____

_____

_____

_____

_____

_____

_____

_____

_____

_____

_____

_____

_____

_____

_____

_____

_____

9. **Who and what am I grateful for in my life, right now? Why?**

What Will You Give Up to Create a Life that you Love?

In order to complete your *steps to success*, you may be realizing that some things have to change in your current life. For example, you may need to study harder, practice more, choose healthier friends, eat healthier foods and exercise, and make better decisions. If you ask successful people what they did to accomplish their goals, I am sure that they'll mention the hard work and determination that was necessary for them to achieve their dreams. They will also tell you that even though it was hard work, and they made sacrifices, it was worth it. No one is an overnight success, and no one does it alone. Success is a journey that takes time and resources. Do not ever forget *who's on your team.*

Exercise:

List three things you may need to give up or change to complete your *steps to success*.

1. _____

   _____

   _____

2. _____

   _____

   _____

3. _____

   _____

   _____

CHAPTER 8

Production Time

Make It Happen—Strategic Goal-Setting

Exercise:

Now that you have your holographic vision, and your vision pages of your ideal self in your ideal life, it's time to make it happen! List up to 3 goals in areas of your life that are important to you, and that, if accomplished, will help you to reach your ideal life and lifestyle. After you have exhausted your ideas, go back, evaluate, and highlight *three* top goals that resonate with you the most. Your goals may encompass some or all of the following areas:

Self-Development

1. _____

_____

_____

2. _____

_____

_____

3. _____

_____

_____

Family

1. _____

_____

_____

2. _____

_____

_____

3. _____

_____

_____

Friends

1. _____

_____

_____

2. _____

_____

_____

3. _____

_____

_____

Spiritual

1. _____

_____

_____

2. _____

_____

_____

3. _____

_____

_____

Academic/Career

1. _____

_____

_____

2. _____

_____

_____

3. _____

_____

_____

Physical and Mental Health

1. _____

_____

_____

2. _____

_____

_____

3. _____

_____

_____

Community Service

1. _____

_____

_____

2. _____

_____

_____

3. _____

_____

_____

Other

1. _____

_____

_____

2. _____

_____

_____

3. _____

_____

_____

Personal Goals

For purposes of this exercise, prioritize and choose **three main goals** for your ideal life, right now.

1. _____

_____

_____

2. _____

_____

_____

3. _____

_____

_____

Then you will create a *holographic vision* statement for each goal. Next, define the *action steps* that you need to take in order to reach each goal. Action steps are a list of solutions that will help you accomplish the goal in a successful manner. Now, list as many action steps as you can think of that may or will work for you. Lastly, make a list of the *resources* you will need to accomplish your goal. Remember, I mentioned this in Chapter 6; you may need to utilize members of your team to help you obtain each goal and become your ideal self.

Example:

Goal: *To use my dance background and skills to form a dance crew with other girls to perform and teach our dances to kids in foster care.*

Category: *Community Service*

Holographic Vision Statement: *I am a healthy and fit teenage girl. I love life and staying active. I have a group of friends who share my love of dance. We have formed a dance crew called "Girl-Swagger." We perform our dances in foster care centers, encouraging other kids to stay active by doing something that is fun and energetic. I love what I do, especially when I see others having fun while dancing and laughing.*

Action Steps:

1. *Recruit friends at school and at my dance studio to see if they want to join the dance crew.*

2. *Find a location to practice our dances.*

3. *Ask my mom or another adult to be our advisor and chaperone.*

4. *Contact the Department of Family and Children's Services to offer our dance services to inspire the kids in their programs.*

5. *Coordinate performance outfits.*

6. *Schedule performance dates.*

7. *DANCE, DANCE, DANCE!*

Resources:

1. Practice locations—dance studio, fitness center, community center, family room, garage, outdoors

2. Music—select the music I love and ask my cousin to make CDs

3. Mom's minivan

4. Department of Family and Children's Services

It is up to you what you will produce for your life. Visualize, create it, and make it happen!

Exercise:

Now it's your turn to turn your dreams into a reality. Let's go!

Goal #1: _____

_____

_____

Category:_____

_____

_____

Action Steps:

1. _____

   _____

   _____

2. _____

   _____

   _____

3. _____

   _____

   _____

4. _____

   _____

   _____

5. _____

_____
_____

6. _____
_____
_____

7. _____
_____
_____

Resources:

1. _____
_____
_____

2. _____
_____
_____

3. _____
_____
_____

4. _____
_____
_____

5. _____
_____
_____

6. _____
_____
_____

7. _____
_____
_____

Goal #2: _____
_____
_____

Category: _____
_____
_____

Action Steps:

1. _____
_____
_____

2. _____

_____

_____

3. _____

_____

_____

4. _____

_____

_____

5. _____

_____

_____

6. _____

_____

_____

7. _____

_____

_____

Resources:

1. _____

_____

_____

2. _____

_____

_____

3. _____

_____

_____

4. _____

_____

_____

5. _____

_____

_____

6. _____

_____

_____

7. _____

_____

_____

Goal #3: _____

_____

_____

Category:_____

_____

_____

Action Steps:

1. _____

_____

_____

2. _____

_____

_____

3. _____

_____

_____

4. _____

_____

_____

5. _____

_____

_____

6. _____

_____

_____

7. _____

_____

_____

Resources:

1. _____

_____

_____

2. _____

_____

_____

3. _____

_____

_____

4. _____

_____

_____

5. _____

_____

_____

6. _____

_____

_____

7. _____

_____

_____

Of your three main goals, which *one* resonates with you the most? Concentrate on that goal right now, the one that is most important to you. Write it down here.

My Most Important Goal Right Now Is:

_____

_____

_____

_____

_____

_____

Why is this goal most important to me?

_____

_____

_____

_____

_____

If your first plan doesn't work, you can modify, enhance, or change it. But do not change your objective. Hold firmly to your holographic vision. Making a mistake or failing in a certain area does not mean you can't be successful. You are bound to make a few mistakes here and there, and obstacles may fall into your path. So, don't be too hard on yourself. You will have to use your creativity to achieve your goal. Remember to utilize your resources; remember who is on your team and then utilize them for helpful advice. And remember, all the greatest individuals in the world have made mistakes, and they have all had to overcome obstacles. I call it *falling forward*. So you'll be in good company.

CHAPTER 9

Have Certainty

Connecting Your Dots and Putting It All Together

Most of us have really great ideas and dreams for ourselves. However, some people don't achieve their dreams because they don't have *clear intentions*. Having clear intentions means being certain about what you want and what you are intending to accomplish. Ask yourself: What do I intend to accomplish today? Now think, "What do I have to do to accomplish my intentions for today?" Do you need to dress in a particular way, do you need to speak to a certain person today, or do you need to complete a task? By knowing what you want and recognizing what you need to do, you have clear intentions.

Did you know that you can create your own *luck*—by being confident in yourself and being clear about your intentions and what you really want? That's right! In your authentic state you have enormous power and abilities, and, now is the time to start creating the life of your dreams! Remember, you're never too young or too old. Don't be your own worst enemy by unconsciously sabotaging and stopping yourself long before you get started—by being overwhelmed, having self-doubt, and not believing in yourself. To be successful in accomplishing your dreams, you have to be confident, have confidence, and project confidence!

Webster's Dictionary defines confidence as:

Trust; reliance

Assurance

Belief in one's own abilities

Belief that another will keep a secret

Something told as a secret (in confidence)

The bottom line is, when you are confident, you *have certainty.*

Do you believe that you are special?

So few of us really believe we are special. Believing that you are special is a prerequisite to becoming your best self. Yes, to become completely comfortable with your natural abilities, your talents, your personality, your special gifts, your innate greatness, and your contribution to the world, you must believe and know that you are *special.* This is the beginning of maintaining your personal power and holding a position in the areas that are important to you: It's your secret to designing the kind of life you were born to live and experience. If you don't think you're special, you will feel unworthy of all the greatness and *girl-swag* that is intended just for you. So, declare your intentions loud and clear to the world, put your plan into action, connect your dots, and make it happen! You will start *creating your own luck through clear intentions.*

Declare Your Intentions

Exercise: Let's start with a simple task of declaring an intention when you wake up tomorrow morning.

Examples:

I intend to smile today and say hello to others as I pass by them.

I intend to take a healthy lunch to school today and eat it with my friends.

I intend to call the Department of Family and Children's Services today to offer our dance services.

I intend to speak clearly and energetically in class today.

I intend to impress my boss by being on time and productive in every assignment.

I intend to use my manners and etiquette skills more today.

I intend to wear a beautiful bright color today.

What do I intend to do today? Write your answer in first person/present tense.

_____

_____

_____

_____

_____

_____

_____

My Seven Simple Steps for Sustainable Success

To be successful in any area that is important to you, a series of effective and efficient actions must be completed. These actions, summarized below, are a roadmap to developing your best self and accomplishing your goals.

1. **Define** in words your *intention—What* do you want? *What* is your heart's desire?

2. **Act**—You've got to get started on what you are intending to do about getting your desires. You've got to *connect your dots and make it happen.*

3. **Plan**—You want to create your plan of action based on your answers to "Who am I?" and "Who am I being?" Then you will be able to hold your position with confidence, certainty and *girl-swag.*

4. **Visualize**—Use your most powerful resource—your mind—to visualize what you intend to create as though you are already experiencing it. Visualize what you will do when you are living your dream. Remember, this is why it is vital that you *define your ideal.* If you can't define it, you can't visualize it or have it. Your Holographic Vision is born from your *intention.*

5. **Intend**—Make your intentions clear. This is your determination about what you want—your dream.

6. **Continue**—Now you're going to continue what you've started by holding on to your crystal-clear vision with certainty. The more you hold on to your vision and think about it, the more attractive it will feel and you will become more energetic and excited about it. It will become more and more attractive to you, and to others around you. The more energy you put into your vision the more it becomes a part of you. The more it becomes *you,* the better chance you will have of *experiencing your vision.*

7. **Completion**—Now you are living what you created in your mind first; you have attained the vision!

*True success of any kind starts in your
mind first—with an intention.*

True success is creative, not competitive.

*You have within you the ability to think a thought
and turn that thought into your reality.*

CHAPTER 10

Command Respect

Turning Up the "IT" Factor and Getting "IT" Done

Remember the "IT" factor I introduced in Chapter 4? I spoke about that special "something" that all individuals have that makes each person special.

I called it the 5 C's:

1. Confidence

2. Character

3. Credibility

4. Connection to others

5. Charisma

Now that you have created your vision, refined your goals, developed your team, planned your action steps, and listed your resources, you are now ready to turn up the "IT" factor—by being *confident*, having a positive *character,* being *credible, connecting* with others, and being *charismatic.*

Chloé Taylor Brown

List at least three to five new positive choices that you will initiate immediately to get you closer to your main dream and your ideal life. *(Let's use the example for creating a dance team for community service: learn new dance techniques, practice more, research other dance teams that have done similar projects, etc.)*

1. _____

_____

_____

2. _____

_____

_____

3. _____

_____

_____

4. _____

_____

_____

5. _____

_____

_____

Create a list of things you absolutely love about yourself and your life— things you want to carry over into your ideal life.

1. _____

   _____

   _____

2. _____

   _____

   _____

3. _____

   _____

   _____

4. _____

   _____

   _____

5. _____

   _____

   _____

6. _____

   _____

   _____

7. _____

   _____

   _____

8. _____

   _____

   _____

9. _____

   _____

   _____

10. _____

    _____

    _____

Incorporating Your Goals and Personal Plan of Action into Your Daily Life

Now that you have developed your "IT" factor—the star that is within you—it is time to work on getting "IT" done. This means setting goals and action steps to accomplish whatever your "IT" is. Your "IT" can be an activity, a project, learning a new language—whatever is important to you. To reach your ideal, you must incorporate the goals and action steps that you have defined into your daily life. If you do not currently use a personal planner, start using one (either an electronic or paper version—whichever works best for you). Working backwards from the date you want to achieve your ideal, record your goals and action steps into your daily planner and on your daily to-do list. This will help to ensure that you are consistently working each day to achieve your ideal.

To do this, take the information from your plan, and do the following:

1. First, define and record the Goals and Action Steps that need to be accomplished **monthly** to reach your ideal. Record these at the beginning of each month. Remember, they really *do* need to be accomplished.

2. Break this down further by identifying and writing down Action Steps that you need to accomplish **weekly** (record these at the beginning of each week).

3. Now, break this down one step further by listing what you need to accomplish **daily** to move yourself toward your goal (put this in your calendar or on your daily to-do list for that specific day).

Monthly, Weekly & Daily Assignments:

Based on the plan you have written, create monthly assignments to get yourself closer to your ideal life.

1. _____

_____

_____

2. _____

_____

_____

3. _____

_____

_____

4. _____

_____

_____

5. _____

_____

_____

6. _____

_____

_____

7. _____

_____

_____

8. _____

_____

_____

9. _____

_____

_____

10. _____

_____

_____

Based on the plan you have written, create weekly assignments to get yourself closer to your monthly goals.

1. _____
_____
_____

2. _____
_____
_____

3. _____
_____

4. _____
_____
_____

5. _____
_____
_____

6. _____
_____
_____

7. _____

8. _____

9. _____

10. _____

Based on the plan you have written, create daily assignments to get yourself closer to your weekly goals.

1. _____

2. _____

3. _____

4. _____

_____

_____

5. _____

_____

_____

Once you have identified daily actions, each morning (or, better yet, the night before) prioritize your daily to-do list by importance, identifying what the one or two most important things are that you must accomplish that day to move you toward your ideal. Now, focus on getting it done. Don't put it off, don't multi-task, and don't do the easy things first! Do the most important things first! You can cross ten tasks off your to-do list, but if you did not accomplish the one or two most important tasks to move toward your ideal, then you were not productive!

Review your strategic plan weekly, and use it to track your **Goals** and **Action Steps** to ensure that you are making daily progress toward accomplishing your desired results.

CHAPTER 11

Expansion

Bigger and Better

I have some good news and some better news. The good news is: You are learning the skills it takes to achieve your personal goals, your ideal self, and how to live life authentically and complete. However, it is not going to happen overnight, or without implementing the plan you have developed for yourself. The better news is: Now you are able to realize your greatest dream, and to turn "IT" into your reality.

Here is an example of *expanding* and getting *bigger and better*. To give you an idea, I am going to use my own story to show you how I have expanded and gotten bigger and better in my own personal and professional life.

Chloe's Story

As a child my first dream was to become a fashion model. By the time I was thirteen I was 5'11" and insecure because I was teased about being tall and thin. But, fortunately a cousin suggested that I could be a model. Honestly, I did not really know what a model was. But because it was a great compliment, and it made me feel good, I decided to explore the possibilities. By the time I was sixteen, I knew I was going to be a model. I started dressing the part, speaking the part, and walking the part. And before long, people started stopping me in the streets and in the malls, asking me if I were a model, which encouraged me all the more. After high school graduation, everyone knew that I was going to be a model.

Chloe's Expansion

1. Went to college and majored in Special Education—until I realized I could actually major in Fashion Merchandising and Design

2. Learned about textiles and fabrics, and constantly studied designers, models, fashion, and photography through magazines and books

3. Started designing and sewing my own fashions

4. Modeled in local fashion shows at my college and small towns, for free

5. Visited fashion houses in New York, and apparel marts in Dallas and Atlanta, to get a better understanding of fashion beyond my homemade clothes

6. Left Mississippi State University to complete my college internship in a retail store in California

7. Signed with an agency in San Francisco and started *expanding* as a fashion model, and *getting bigger and better*

8. Signed with an agency in Milan, Italy, and worked in Paris, Frankfurt, Barcelona, Atlanta, Chicago, and New York

9. Worked with Armani, Versace, Escada, Dolce & Gabbana, Revlon, and others

10. Returned to Mississippi State University years later to complete my degree, but was challenged in passing college algebra, but I did not allow that to block or top me

11. Took a business writing class when I realized I had major blocks in algebra, which rekindled my love of books and led to a love and passion for researching, writing, and inspirational speaking.

12. Created and established my personal and professional business as a lifestyle enhancement coach

13. Created my first self-help product for girls on body image and self-esteem from my business writing class assignment

14. Published my first book *Getting Ready Chloe-Style: Perfecting Your Authentic Image*

15. *Now I am living my dream.* I continue to model, but not on the runway. And I have expanded on my childhood dream by inspiring, encouraging, and empowering young girls to follow their dreams and passions as my cousin inspired and encouraged me when I was thirteen.

16. TO BE CONTINUED...as I continue to expand and get *bigger* and *better*!

Feeding the Dream

As you can see, nothing happens overnight, and dreams can take you in a new direction in your life. You may start out with a small idea, which may lead to various directions along your path. But if you "stick to it" you can end up exceeding your expectations. However, it is important to create your holographic vision, and to explore and expand it. Remember who you are, remember who is on your team, and identify your resources. It takes time and quite a bit of hard work; but if you feed your dream, your dream will grow and develop into the most beautiful, amazing "IT"—and when this happens, it will appear as though you are hardly working. Remember this, ladies: ***The dream wants you as much as you want the dream.***

CHAPTER 12

The Final Accomplishment

You in Your Ideal Life!

Now that you have completed all the required steps to determine your ideal and to be a girl with swag—I want you to describe vividly and boldly what you have created for yourself—in the present tense. Be detailed and descriptive. Revel in this! Use your GIRL-SWAG. Experience the feelings, see all the colors, and smell all the fragrances. Hear what is being said around you and about you as you shine with the accomplishments that you have created from your mind.

Pay attention to all the amazing people who want to be around you, who want to be connected with you, and who want to join your team—as you become more and more your real, authentic self.

_____

_____

_____

_____

_____

_____

_____

_____

_____

_____

_____

_____

_____

_____

_____

_____

_____

_____

_____

_____

_____

_____

_____

_____

_____

_____

_____

_____

Taste the life you desire and deserve...
IT'S YOURS TO LIVE.

My Life Experiences Page
(Photos of Me Living My Girl-Swag Accomplishments)

My Life Experiences Page
(Photos of Me Living My Girl-Swag Accomplishments)

My Life Experiences Page
(Photos of Me Living My Girl-Swag Accomplishments)

My Life Experiences Page
(Photos of Me Living My Girl-Swag Accomplishments)

MY WISH FOR YOU!

Dear Girls with Swag,

You are amazing! I wrote this book so that you would believe in *you* as much as I believe in you. I want you to know that you are very valuable. You are worth having an idea, turning that idea into a dream, and creating your ideal life from that idea.

Remember this, if you want to do something truly wonderful for yourself and for the world, determine your ideal and make the most of yourself. Within the essence of who you are lies the power to change your life. It all begins with just one thought.

At all times try to maintain a positive attitude and mood. It's up to you— you're in control. Determine that you will not allow negative people and other outside influences to interfere or to control your attitude. Stay away from people and things that bring your spirit and mood down.

Ladies, don't expect to get a lot in return if all you're giving is just enough to get by. On the other hand, if you're being effective and efficient— giving it your all and doing all you can do—you will be rewarded for your efforts, and sooner rather than later.

I cannot stress enough how important it's going to be that you hold on to your faith in yourself and in your vision during this process. And remember, it's a *creative* process. There is *nothing competitive* about your goals, your dreams and your ideal. Believe that. See that.

Put your time, your energy, your money, and your whole heart into *your dream— your determined ideal, and what you want to accomplish—* and believe without a doubt that you can do it. Also, you'll want to connect with people who have already accomplished their goals; goals that are similar to yours, as well as goals that are different. Know that you are loved, and that others have confidence in you and in your abilities. Remember your past successes, and build on them. Always acknowledge yourself when you achieve your goals. Also, remember to acknowledge your friends and peers as they accomplish their goals— and watch your confidence soar.

I'm thinking BIG with you!

—Chloé Taylor Brown